The Awesome Prayer of Jesus

A Portrait of Divine Unity

Jean Robert Lainé, Ph.D.

ABOUT THIS PUBLICATION

First Edition

Copyright © 2020 Jean Robert Lainé.
All rights reserved.

Published in 2020 by Jean Robert Lainé
Oklahoma City, Oklahoma

No part of this book may be reproduced without the publisher's permission, except when quoted in scholarly studies, speeches, or similar settings. For permission, Contact us at **Laineed2017@gmail.com.**

Scripture quotations are from the Holy Bible, New International Version (NIV). Copyright © 1973, 1978, 1984, 2011, Biblica, Inc.™ Used by permission. All rights reserved worldwide.

Title: The Awesome Prayer of Jesus: A Portrait of Divine Unity

Cover Design: Amazon KDP Cover Creator

Library of Congress Control Number:
2020903457
ISBN: 9781733764889
Paperback

Table of Contents

DEDICATION vi
ACKNOWLEDGEMENTS vii
INTRODUCTION viii
CHAPTER ONE 1
   A MUTUAL REQUEST 1
CHAPTER TWO 7
   THE AUTHORITY OF JESUS CHRIST 7
CHAPTER THREE 14
   ETERNAL LIFE 14
CHAPTER FOUR 19
   GOD'S GLORY ON EARTH 19
CHAPTER FIVE 23
   ETERNAL GLORY 23
CHAPTER SIX 27
   CHRIST REVEALED THE FATHER 27
CHAPTER SEVEN 32
   THEY ACCEPTED JESUS' MESSAGE 32
CHAPTER EIGHT 37
   JESUS EVALUATED HIS MISSION 37
CHAPTER NINE 42

JESUS PRAYED FOR THOSE WHO BELIEVED HIS MESSAGE............ 42

CHAPTER TEN 49
PERFECT HARMONY 49
END OF JESUS' EARTHLY MISSION 53

CHAPTER TWELVE 59
THERE IS PROTECTION IN JESUS' NAME 59

CHAPTER THIRTEEN 63
JESUS GIVES JOY 63

CHAPTER FOURTEEN 67
JESUS IS AWARE OF OUR SUFFERING 67

CHAPTER FIFTEEN 70
JESUS PRAYED FOR OUR PROTECTION 70

CHAPTER SIXTEEN 72
WE DON'T BELONG HERE 72

CHAPTER SEVEN 75
GOD SETS US APART 75

CHAPTER EIGHTEEN 78
JESUS' MISSION IS NOT OVER 78

CHAPTER NINETEEN 83
JESUS' SANCTIFICATION BENEFITS US 83

CHAPTER TWENTY 86
JESUS PRAYED FOR ALL BELIEVERS 86

CHAPTER TWENTY-ONE 93
JESUS SHARED HIS GLORY WITH US 93
CHAPTER TWENTY-TWO 96
COMPLETE UNITY 96
CHAPTER TWENTY-THREE 100
JESUS' ETERNAL GLORY 100
CHAPTER TWENTY-FOUR 105
IF WE KNOW JESUS, WE KNOW THE FATHER . 105
CHAPTER TWENTY-FIVE 111
JESUS MADE THE FATHER KNOWN 111
ABOUT THE AUTHOR 114
BOOKS BY THIS AUTHOR 116

DEDICATION

I dedicate this book to all who have put their trust in Jesus Christ- the Messiah.

ACKNOWLEDGEMENTS

I thank Cheryl, my wife, for supporting my idea of writing a book on Jesus' prayer in John 17. I also thank Fonda Watkins, my sister in the LORD, for reading one of my many drafts and give me some positive feedback.

INTRODUCTION

No one knows the heavenly Father better than the Son, so if we want to know the heavenly Father, we need to go through Jesus the Son.

This book introduces you to the most incredible prayer Jesus has ever prayed on earth. Jesus' prayer in John 17 will open your mind to understanding the divine unity that exists among the Godhead: the Father, the Son, and the Holy Spirit. It is a profound reflection of God's glory.

As you meditate on each verse and sentence in this book, I pray that you will feel the presence of God. Your life should never be the same when you are finished reading this book.

CHAPTER ONE

A MUTUAL REQUEST

"Father, the hour has come. Glorify your Son, that your Son may glorify you." - John 17:1 NIV

Everything Jesus came to accomplish was about to be fulfilled. The stakes were extremely high. The stage was set, and the world's cameras were on Jesus. Both the earthly and heavenly hosts were ready for the curtains to be rolled back. This movie features Jesus, the Son of Yahweh, our true God. Imagine the emotional state in which Jesus was when He finally saw the light at the end of the tunnel. Of course, Jesus knew all along how everything was going to end.

When you are assigned a particular project, all your energy goes into executing it to perfection. You know the outcome will bring joy and satisfaction to your boss, but you cannot get too excited yet, because you still have a long process to go through. Although Jesus was equal to God, He humbled Himself and accepted a challenge that would cause Him to suffer the worst punishment ever so that God could demonstrate His love toward us.

Jesus took a deep breath and said, "Father, the hour has come." It does not matter how long you have been suffering; there will come a time when you will be able to see the end of your trauma. Jesus did not give up. He hung on until He could see the end of His mission on earth.

If victory is your goal, you cannot abandon ship when things get tough. Had Jesus given up during His trials, we would not have had the opportunity to reconcile with God. It took Jesus a long time before His hour came. Wait for your hour to arrive. Though it delays, it will surely come; not one day will pass.

Jesus is the reflection of God's glory. If Jesus had not overcome the power of darkness, Satan would have triumphed over God's plan. Since Satan set out to overthrow God, He had to find a way to defeat Satan. He had to restore eternal life, which Satan had destroyed when he deceived Adam and Eve in the Garden of Eden.

By glorifying Jesus, God's glory became evident. Satan had a secret project to eliminate God's plan for humanity, but God overtly showcased His power by sending His Son to foil Satan's evil scheme.

As the Father glorifies His Son, He too is glorified. In

this verse, His prayer's introduction shows us the spiritual reciprocity between Him and the Father. We must know that God takes pleasure in us as well. For that reason, God sent Jesus to die for us because our destruction would not glorify God. We are the object of God's glory. It is marvelous to see how it all plays out. God has planned everything to be how it is, even the wicked, for the day of destruction.

CHAPTER TWO

THE AUTHORITY OF JESUS CHRIST

"For you granted him authority over all people that he might give eternal life to all those you have given him." - John 17:2 NIV

Jesus was not an ordinary missionary sent from heaven. He was endowed with all authority from the Father to do everything He came to do. It was not an accident. God planned every step of Jesus' mission according to His will.

If you have any doubt about the truth of the Gospel, listen carefully to the voice of Jesus. He said that "His Father granted Him authority over all people." We are not talking about a prophet's limited power, as many would want you to believe. We are talking about total control over everything that has breath, whether on earth, under the seas, and in the galaxies. There is nothing that does not fall under the direct authority of Jesus. It does not matter how powerful someone is; they are under Jesus' complete control.

What is so crucial in this aspect of Jesus' prayer is that the heavenly Father gave Jesus the authority to give eternal life. If you knew someone who has the authority to grant you everlasting life, what would you be willing to pay them for it? Jesus is such a person. He has the power to give you eternal life free of charge. You have nothing to pay. If you are willing to surrender your heart to Jesus right now, He will instantly provide you with eternal life.

Jesus had an extraordinary assignment. His mission was to save the world by reconciling people with the Father. He came as the Savior for the entire humanity.

What you need to grasp here is that the Father had reached an agreement with His Son to come down to earth in the form of a human being to accomplish something that would reverse the evil act of Satan. Jesus' birth, death, and resurrection put in motion a plan that Satan can never foil. As far as God is concerned, Satan is already defeated. There is nothing he can do to defeat Jesus. It is a matter of time. After that, Satan will receive his just punishment for his meddling in God's eternal plan.

Jesus' death and resurrection made it possible for all to receive eternal life because Jesus' authority has included everyone. The only thing that can stop you from receiving eternal life is your will. God gives Jesus power over you, but the choice is yours to make. The fact that God has the last word, your best bet is to surrender your will to God and allow Him to grant you eternal life through His Son Jesus Christ. You do not have to take my word for it. Listen to Jesus. He said that He had the authority to give eternal life, and such power came directly from His Father, who sent Him to carry out such a difficult mission on earth. That was a challenging assignment, but He did it for you and me.

CHAPTER THREE

ETERNAL LIFE

"Now this is eternal life: that they know you, the only true God, and Jesus Christ, whom you have sent." - John 17:3 NIV

Have you ever wondered what it takes to have eternal life? Jesus spells out the very secret here in His fervent prayer.

Eternal life starts with knowing God. There are many gods in this world or many things that people worship as gods. Jesus wanted to make it clear that He was not referring to a fake god somewhere. Jesus referred to Yahweh - the only true God. If you want to know the true God, you need to make acquaintance with the God to whom Jesus was praying. First, Jesus referred to the only true God as His Father in the opening prayer. Jesus was not referring to an unknown being or a high being as some people often refer to God because they do not have a relationship with Him like Jesus does.

We cannot obtain Eternal life through some vague knowledge of an unknown god. The heavenly Father choreographed the eternal life that Jesus carried out. Such a spiritual exploit was not evolved by natural selection or the big bang theory, as some scientists may want you to believe. Eternal life is part of God's plan for the universe, and He took great care to ensure that Satan, the archenemy, got defeated forever by the birth, death, and resurrection of Jesus.

Eternal life is obtained through the knowledge of God by embracing Jesus Christ, the Son of God. Without Jesus Christ, eternal life is not attainable. Jesus is the means through which God chose to defeat Satan. If you refuse to acknowledge Jesus' ultimate sacrifice, there is no more sacrifice left for you. Whether you accept Jesus now or later, you have a life-transforming decision to make. You will have to make it now or later. If you have already made such a crucial decision, count yourself among the blessed ones because there is nothing more glorious than having the hope of eternal life through Jesus Christ the Savior.

CHAPTER FOUR

GOD'S GLORY ON EARTH

"I have brought you glory on earth by finishing the work you gave me to do." - John 17:4 NIV

If you have ever finished something dauntingly challenging, you can imagine the satisfaction Jesus felt in His conversation with His Father. I use "conversation" here to denote the ease between Jesus and His Father.

When we pray, we should relax and allow the Holy Spirit to establish a sense of ease and camaraderie between the heavenly Father and us because Jesus provides us with a special connection through His death and resurrection. We can come to God boldly in the name of Jesus.

Finishing the work is critical here. God did not call us to do half of the work. He called us to finish the job. Jesus traced an excellent example for us to follow. Jesus' task was not easy, yet

He finished it. He had to depend on His Father for strength every step of the way. On our journey through life, we, too, will continue to face temptation every step of the way, but we will overcome our obstacles by God's grace.

We should not give up sharing our testimonies because we bring glory to Him as we do. Jesus came to establish the path of eternal life, but we continue to showcase His work through our lifestyle and testimonies. We should not be afraid to share God's love with others because, in so doing, more people will know God.

No matter how difficult it may be, stay on task. Your hour will soon come when you will be able to see the fruits of your labor. Just like Jesus, you must endure this world's hardship. But, be of good cheer, for your sorrows are temporary. Eternal life awaits you in heaven. Soon and very soon, you will be with God in glory.

CHAPTER FIVE

ETERNAL GLORY

"And now, Father, glorify me in your presence with the glory I had with you before the world began" (John 17:5 NIV).

Jesus abandoned His eternal glory temporarily to fulfill His Father's wishes. As the time was approaching for Jesus the Messiah to finish His earthly mission and return to the Father, He began to acknowledge the glory He had with His Father before creating the universe.

It is essential to know that Jesus Christ is God. He came as the Messiah to save us from our sins. As such, He had to humble Himself by accepting to become a man. Being a man, He was subject to physical pain and this world's sufferings. He did this for you and me.

Although Jesus knew that His Father was always there, He wanted to be glorified in His Father's presence. He needed His Father's reassurance as He was about to suffer the worst physical and emotional trauma ever! It is okay for you to call on God in trials. God knows your situation and wants you to have His complete reassurance that He will never forsake you. You are never alone when you walk with God, even though you may feel lonely sometimes.

Jesus drew from His own experience with the Father. Before the world began, Jesus Christ had a relationship with the Father, so He was able to refer to that relationship. What is your point of reference? Did you have an encounter with God that you can refer to in times of trouble? Do not hesitate to remind God of those past moments, even though God knows everything. A reference to an experience is a morale booster. It helps us remember what God did in the past so we can continue to trust God in the present circumstances. David did the same when he faced Goliath. He referred to God's miraculous protection from dangerous wild animals.

CHAPTER SIX

CHRIST REVEALED THE FATHER

"I have revealed you to those whom you gave me out of the world. They were yours; you gave them to me and they have obeyed your word." - John 17:6 NIV

No one can know the Father without Jesus Christ's revelation. So, Jesus Christ came to introduce the Father to the world.

Christ had a particular mission. But, first, He came to make the Father known, and for Him to accomplish such a big task, He had to shed His blood to redeem us.

Remember, the world, from the beginning, had belonged to God. However, something cataclysmic occurred in the Garden of Eden that altered the divine path God had created. Therefore, the initial plan of God was put in peril by Lucifer, who is now Satan or the evil one.

Jesus came to undo all the plans of Satan. Christ's birth gave him the natural right to claim Adam's lawful rights as a human. Without Christ's incarnation, He could not have claimed authority over Adam's power. To rule the earth was a right that God had given Adam at the time of creation. But, since he lost it through disobedience, only someone who was without sin could claim it. And that someone is Jesus Christ, the Son of Yahweh.

Christ's death and resurrection gave him the

authority to overcome death. His victory over death made it possible for us to have victory over death as well, even though we must die in the flesh to have access to it. Physical death, for us, is a transition to eternal life. Without physical death, we cannot transition to eternity. Jesus Christ demonstrated His victory over death to guarantee that we, too, will overcome death in the end.

Today we can know God by obeying Christ's word. He said that He is "the way the truth and the life" (John

14:6). Therefore, by surrendering our hearts to Him, we have eternal life. As a result, we can now say we know the Father through Jesus Christ, hence God's revelation to us through His Son.

CHAPTER SEVEN

THEY ACCEPTED JESUS' MESSAGE

"Now they know that everything you have given me comes from you." - John 17:7 NIV

The disciples knew that Jesus was not making things up in that they realized that He was the Messiah. Jesus did not come on His own accord. He came to fulfill a particular mission whose objective was to reconcile the world with Yahweh. For the disciples to experience the transformational message of Jesus Christ, they had to believe what Jesus Christ was sharing with them.

The message of Jesus is only compelling if we accept it as truth from the Father. We must put our faith in Jesus' sacrifice to reap the spiritual benefits of His mission. As the author of the book of Hebrews said in chapter 6 verse 11, "And without faith, it is impossible to please God because anyone who comes to him must believe that he exists and that he rewards those who earnestly seek him."

Every idea Jesus Christ shared about heaven came from the Father. Jesus wanted to make it clear beyond a shadow of a doubt what His mission was all about, and He managed to convince His disciples about it. In other words, Jesus Christ experienced total success as a messenger sent by the Father. His disciples realized that He was not an impostor.

We must ensure that we present the Gospel with clarity so that others can come to know God through our message. When preaching the Good News, we must not promote ourselves. Jesus Christ did not promote Himself while He was on earth. Instead, He spent His missionary tenure teaching about heavenly things. Therefore, we ought to spend our time on earth promoting God and those things that have eternal impact. Something that will not stand the test of time is a waste of time. When tested, they will burn up. Now, I am not saying that you need to neglect your duties as a member of society. On the contrary, you need to continue contributing to the community as a citizen without losing sight of your divine purpose.

CHAPTER EIGHT

JESUS EVALUATED HIS MISSION

"For I gave them the words you gave me and they accepted them. They knew with certainty that I came from you, and they believed that you sent me." - John 17:8 NIV

Jesus did not share His message. He was commissioned with a special message from His

Father, and He delivered it with fidelity.

If you are called to preach the Gospel, you need to be sure that you preach it faithfully. God did not call you to share your message. Instead, He called you to share His message with those who are perishing.

Jesus knew that He was successful because He did what His Father sent Him to do. If you do what God sent you to do, you do not have to worry, even though you may face fierce opposition. Even though His Father sent

Him, that did not shield Him from constant attack from Satan, so do not doubt God's calling upon your life just because things are not going smoothly. God did not promise to shield us from temptation. But, He promised not to abandon us while we are going through temptation.

Jesus was able to evaluate the success of His mission because He knew what His disciples were thinking. Jesus did not have to wait for anyone to testify. Jesus' disciples knew with certainty that God sent Him to do everything that He did. Today do you doubt that God sent Jesus in the flesh to save you? Just like the disciples, you, too, need to come to a complete understanding of who Jesus is. You need to know with certainty that Jesus is the Messiah and that He is who He says He is.

By believing one hundred percent that the heavenly Father sent Jesus Christ, we have no room left in our minds for uncertainty. Such rock-solid confession is the crucial foundation for our hope of glory. If the heavenly Father did not send Jesus, He would be the greatest impostor ever. And everything that we know about Christianity today would be false. Jesus' prayer has confirmed once and for all that He was not fake. Based on Jesus' revelation through His intimate conversation with His Father, we now can trust in Him to save us.

CHAPTER NINE

JESUS PRAYED FOR THOSE WHO BELIEVED HIS MESSAGE

"I pray for them. I am not praying for the world, but for those you have given me, for they are yours" *(John 17:9).*

While God's love extends to the whole world, He has a special appreciation for those who have surrendered their lives to Him. When you say yes to Jesus, you become part of a divine plan. You are counted among those who have been called to live forever with God.

Jesus prayed for those who accepted Him because He knew that they would endure a lot for Him. Although we know God, we are not exempt from the present sufferings. Our sufferings will end when we finally get to heaven.

If you have surrendered your life to God, you should know that you are not alone in the fight. God's eyes are constantly on you. Do not give up as you endure your adversity. Remain faithful to God during your hardship. Satan will do everything in his power to make you lose heart but continue to trust God with all your heart no matter what.

Jesus was not praying for the world because the world cannot receive this type of blessing. Some opportunities are only accessible to God's people. People who are not living for God cannot have access to those kinds of benefits.

When you pray, ask God to give you all the blessings that He has for His people. Know that God has many opportunities for you. We cannot live a blessed life if we do not know what God has for us. For example, suppose someone has deposited a billion dollars in a bank account in your name. You have spent years living in poverty because you have no clue that you are so wealthy. And one day, someone came to you and said, "You do know that you are rich, right? You answered, "What?" The person responded, "Yes, you are filthy rich." And they went on and said, "You just need to acknowledge the gift and go to the bank to claim it." It is the way it is with eternal life in Christ. Jesus paid the total price for us. All we need to do is to accept Him as our Lord and Savior to have access to everything that God has for us.

God's people are extraordinary because they are on the side of God. Jesus was happy because He realized that His mission was about to finish. So, Jesus made salvation available to all. He rejoiced over those He had a chance to touch personally during His short stay on earth.

Today you have the same privilege as those for whom Jesus was praying if you have made Him your Lord and Savior. You do not have to be afraid to approach God with your problems because He knows who you are and what you are going through. So be ready to call on the name of Jesus in times of trouble. He loves you so much and wants to come to your rescue. Jesus is interceding for you, even now.

CHAPTER TEN

PERFECT HARMONY

"All I have is yours, and all you have is mine. And glory has come to me through them." - John 17:10 NIV

In this verse, Jesus made it clear that He and His Father are one. There is no division between the Son and the heavenly Father. They are co-independent. Each entity has complete access to everything in the kingdom. The closest earthly example of this type of unity is a marriage built on solid biblical principles. They are co-owners of everything they have. That goes for their bodies as well.

There is unity among the Father, the Son, and the Holy Spirit in the heavenly realm. Therefore, Yahweh orchestrated everything to ensure spiritual harmony in the Godhead.

   This verse reinforces Jesus' authority in verse 2, where the Father has granted Him all power to save. By this equal ownership, Jesus can make decisions. If we ask Jesus for something we need, which is within God's will, He can reach out and help us without any restriction.

Although we may not claim equal access to everything God has, as in the case of Jesus, we have some access to unlimited provisions because of our relationship with the heavenly Father. We have access to what God has because we belong to Him. If we belong to the King of kings, we are, therefore, princes and princesses. It is through this lens we can understand the amount of access we have to what God possesses.

Based on this spiritual insight, we should not consider ourselves as paupers. Instead, we should rejoice in the fact that our God has unlimited resources in every sphere of life, whether it be authority over the power of darkness, power to rule over Satan, and help to get things done for the glory of God.

CHAPTER ELEVEN

END OF JESUS' EARTHLY MISSION

"I will remain in the world no longer, but they are still in the world, and I am coming to you. Holy Father, protect them by the power of your name, the name you gave me, so that they may be one as we are one." – John 17:11 NIV

Anticipating the end of His earthly mission and His eventual return to the Father, Jesus was thinking about His disciples and all those who would put their trust in Him.

Jesus had a specific duty. He was on earth to bring salvation to everyone through His birth, death, and resurrection. His mission was not designed to be permanent. It had a beginning and an end. The mission of the Church is to continue spreading the Good News of the kingdom. The Church has nothing to fear because we have God's protection in the name of

Jesus. As Jesus was preparing to return to His Father, He knew life on earth would not be easy for His followers. Those who are committed to serving the Lord Jesus as their Lord and Savior must endure daily temptation. Satan, God's number one enemy, is doing everything to destroy the hope of eternal life. He does that by sowing the seed of doubt in believers' minds.

As Christ's followers, we must resist Satan's attacks and press on toward our goals. We must share our faith with others so that they, too, can put their trust in Jesus the Messiah. Jesus is aware of our daily struggle. He will not abandon us in the fight. Because Jesus is with the Father, He can defend us before the heavenly Father when Satan is trying to accuse us. He is our Supreme Judge.

Someday, we will be with the heavenly Father, where Jesus is now. So let us not lose heart as we face daily temptation. We are in the world, but our minds are not focused on earthly things because we are going to heaven, where there will be no pain or suffering.

Today, salvation is available to all. No further sacrifice is necessary. It is a matter of our will and commitment. We must choose to put our trust in the shed blood of Jesus to receive salvation. We can obtain salvation through faith in the finished work of Jesus on the cross. But, unfortunately, we will never be able to work for it.

Through God's grace, we are united with God. Jesus'

prayer is that we become one with the Father just as He is one with Him.

CHAPTER TWELVE

THERE IS PROTECTION IN JESUS' NAME

"While I was with them, I protected them and kept them safe by that name you gave me. None has been lost except the one doomed to destruction so that Scripture would be fulfilled." - John 17:12 NIV

It is not without reason that king Solomon said in Proverbs 18 verse 10, "The name of the Lord is a fortified tower; the righteous run to it and are safe." There is power in the name of Jesus. More importantly, there is salvation in the name of Jesus. As a matter of fact, in the Hebrew language, Jesus or Yeshua means Yahweh is salvation.

There is no other name that is more powerful than the name of Jesus. In His name, we can overcome the power of darkness.

While Jesus was on earth, His disciples used His name as a shield. Judas did not have that protection because his life's purpose was to fulfill the Scripture. Someone had to betray the Son of God for Him to die for us. God, in His sovereignty, had decided before the creation of the world how salvation was going to be made available to all humanity, and Judas was part of that divine process of salvation. We need to know and remember that the Sovereign God is in control of everyone's destiny.

Nothing can be done outside His sovereignty and complete awareness.

As far as we are concerned, if we surrender our lives to God by accepting Jesus as our Lord and Savior, we can count on God's protection. God will keep us safe in the name of Jesus. Therefore, Satan has no power over us.

CHAPTER THIRTEEN

JESUS GIVES JOY

"I am coming to you now, but I say these things while I am still in the world, so that they may have the measure of my joy within them." – John 17:13 NIV

Jesus was ready to join His Father in heaven, so He did not have any reason to mention all these things in His prayer. However, He knew that His disciples would need a source of joy and inspiration. When we are going through tough times, we need a point of reference. In other words, we need something beyond our circumstances to anchor our faith to hold on to life. Without such hope, we have nothing to fight for. That is why so many people choose to end their lives because they cannot see any reason to continue living.

Jesus has given us so much for which to live. So then, He turned our attention to the heavenly Father. There is so much hope in Jesus and what He stands for. When we think about eternity and everything that the Holy Scriptures promise about life with the heavenly Father, we have a whole lot of hope and joy.

Today, if you are going through hardship, please draw from the measure of joy that Jesus has provided for you. Jesus died so that you could have joy. There is hope for you, my friend, despite your current situation. Put your hope in Jesus because He cares a great deal for you. Do not give up hope. Keep on breathing. You can still experience a breakthrough, even at the last minute. Jesus is interceding on your behalf because He loves you a lot. He wants you to experience the true joy that comes from the heavenly Father, who loves you so much.

CHAPTER FOURTEEN

JESUS IS AWARE OF OUR SUFFERING

"I have given them your word, and the world has hated them, for they are not of the world any more than I am of the world." – John 17:14 NIV

When you surrender your heart to Jesus Christ, you decide to live a life that focuses on eternity. By your decision to walk with the LORD, you now have a different view of life. You should see yourself as this world's temporary resident.

From an immigration viewpoint, temporary residents do not entirely belong to the country in which they live. Therefore, their rights are limited until they have obtained citizenship through naturalization.

Christians should not feel too comfortable on this planet from a spiritual dimension because this life is not the real deal. Eternity is the ultimate focus of the Church of Jesus Christ.

If you love Jesus, Satan will do everything in his power to persecute you. There is a real battle going on among God's people and those who are following Satan. Because you belong to Jesus, that does not mean that you will not face persecution. Nevertheless, you can count on the heavenly Father for daily protection.

CHAPTER FIFTEEN

JESUS PRAYED FOR OUR PROTECTION

"My prayer is not that you take them out of the world but that you protect them from the evil one." – John 17:15 NIV

You may be tempted to pray for complete exemption from hardship, but it is not promised. If you are born again, you can count on

God's protection. If you pray for exemption, you are not praying according to God's will. To make Jesus known, we must stay in the world to spread the Good News of the kingdom. We cannot jump ship amid persecution. We need to ask God to protect us during attacks to continue the Church's mission. There is a lot at stake. There are many lost souls to be saved.

Take courage that the time of our deliverance is near. We are not going to suffer forever.

CHAPTER SIXTEEN

WE DON'T BELONG HERE

"They are not of the world, even as I am not of it." – John 17:16 NIV

Again, Jesus emphasized His heavenly citizenship and that of His disciples. The reality is that we do not belong here. We are just passing through. When we compare an earthly lifespan with eternal life, it is insignificant. Through Jesus, we have access to eternity. Jesus' ultimate mission was to provide us with eternal life. The concept of living forever lost its meaning when Adam and Eve chose to disobey the Creator.

The way we live determines our focus. While we need to remain involved as responsible citizens, we need to ensure that our lifestyle shows that we belong to an eternal kingdom while ensuring that we reach our full potential in everything we do. Moreover, we should make the best of our time here by building for eternity through our service and financial contributions toward the advancement of God's kingdom.

CHAPTER SEVENTEEN

GOD SETS US APART

"Sanctify them by the truth; your word is truth." – John 17:17 NIV

The truth sets the Church of Jesus Christ apart from other institutions on earth. The Church is not built on a myth. She is built on Jesus Christ, who is the Chief Cornerstone. That is why the

Church is called the bride of Christ.

The truth is the ultimate knowledge and understanding of who Jesus is. This truth about Jesus Christ has the power to consecrate you for the service of the LORD. You can never be the same again after your encounter with Yahweh, the God of Abraham, the God of Isaac, the God of Jacob, and the God of Israel.

God's word is truth. There is no falsehood in what the Bible says about Jesus Christ.

God has indeed demonstrated His unconditional love for us by sending His Son Jesus Christ to die in our place. If you believe this biblical account and put your complete trust in Jesus Christ as your Lord and Savior, you have been set apart by God based on this truth. In so doing, you are among those who will spend their eternity with the heavenly Father in the New Jerusalem. God has declared you sanctified because you have accepted the truth about Jesus the Messiah.

CHAPTER EIGHTEEN

JESUS' MISSION IS NOT OVER

"As you sent me into the world, I have sent them into the world." – John 17:18 NIV

Jesus laid the Church's foundation by offering His own life on the cross, but there is still more to be done to fulfill the mission's intent. If no one knows about what Jesus Christ did on the cross, His death is in vain.

That was one reason Jesus did not ask His Father to take His disciples away from this world. Instead, He only prayed for their protection. Jesus' death on the cross was a game-changer. After the debacle of Adam and Eve in the Garden of Eden, Yahweh has given humans a golden opportunity to reconcile with the Creator. The Good News of the kingdom was something that Jesus wanted His disciple to spread throughout the world, starting in Judea, Samaria, and the rest of the world. This mandate is for every believer. We, the followers of Christ, are responsible for telling others how much the heavenly Father loves them by sending Jesus Christ to die on the cross for them. Just as the Father sent Jesus, Jesus has commissioned His followers to spread the Good News. People need to know that God, through Jesus Christ, is willing to save them from their sins. They ought to know there is life beyond the grave in that they can live forever with God in the New Jerusalem.

If you have surrendered your life to Jesus Christ as your Lord and Savior, know that you are God's witness. You may not have God's calling to travel the world to spread the Gospel, but you can still be helpful in God's kingdom. Try and find ways to contribute toward building for eternity through your participation in the local Church. Live your life in such a way that those who are not believers can put their trust in Jesus Christ.

Let your lifestyle be a lamp for all the world to see.

CHAPTER NINETEEN

JESUS' SANCTIFICATION BENEFITS US

"For them I sanctify myself, that they too may be truly sanctified."
– John 17:19 NIV

Jesus' commitment to the mission His Father gave Him was remarkable. He was not here to please

Himself. He was dedicated to doing what His Father sent Him to do. Jesus consecrated Himself so that we, too, could be consecrated. He did not spare any energy. He gave His all for the mission.

Despite the temptation to neglect the things of God, we need to live our lives for God. We know that the heavenly Father sanctifies, but we need to grow in maturity as we experience the Christian faith.
Sanctification is both a finished act and a work in progress. On the one hand,

God has declared us sanctified when we accept the truth about His Son. On the other hand, we continue to experience sanctification by living for Jesus in this fallen world. We will not share the fullness of sanctification until God glorified our mortal bodies. Praise God that He sanctified us by faith through grace based on what Jesus accomplished on the cross.

CHAPTER TWENTY

JESUS PRAYED FOR ALL BELIEVERS

"My prayer is not for them alone. I pray also for those who will believe in me through their message, that all of them may be one, Father, just as you are in me and I am in you. May they also be in us so that the world may believe that you have sent me." – John 17: 20 and 21 NIV

What makes Jesus' prayer extraordinary is that it is all-encompassing. It is inclusive. Jesus was not just thinking about His disciples. He was thinking about His disciples and all future Christians who will later believe in the Gospel. That is a remarkable prayer in that Jesus thought of us, even before we were born. We need to know that the Creator knew about us before creation. We are unique in God's eyes.

Today we can count on this prayer when we face trials. But, first, we need to acknowledge God's provision. God, in His omniscience, has provided everything we need to make it through this world. He knew every difficult moment that we are going to endure. There is nothing that God in His sovereignty cannot see.

We tend to panic when we face challenging moments because we are not fully aware of God's provision and protection.

As you journey through life, remember God had you in mind before you were born. So, your current situation is completely covered. God has got your back!

Jesus wants us to grasp the whole message of unity in the Godhead and the spiritual impact on us believers. We become one with God by Jesus' union with the Father. That is a special connection that is only possible through a born-again experience. It is one of the marvelous mysteries of the Church. People who are not committed to serving God cannot understand this union.

Considering our relationship with God, we are always in God's presence. We can never be alone when we walk with God. If by any chance you feel lonely, ask God to renew your spirit. We do not always feel the full impact of salvation in our emotions and bodies. Our spirits are the ultimate recipients of salvation. The only part of you that is wholly saved is your spirit. That is why you sometimes struggle to remain faithful to God despite your knowledge and understanding of God. When God glorifies you, every part of you will be saved. In other words, your body, soul, and spirit will be totally surrendered to God. From time to time, you must remind your body that it is the temple of the Holy Spirit. When bad ideas cross your mind, your emotional realm, you need to surrender them to God. Remind your mind that you belong to Yahweh, the Almighty God.

Our Christian experience is vital for the world because unbelievers may trust God by observing how we live our lives. When they see God's love in us, they too will acknowledge that Jesus is the Son of God. They will believe that the Father has sent Him to save us. It is something that Jesus prayed that would happen following His ascension to heaven.

CHAPTER TWENTY-ONE

JESUS SHARED HIS GLORY WITH US

"I have given them the glory that you gave me, that they may be one as we are one." – John 17:22 NIV

Jesus wasn't satisfied with just rescuing us from eternal death. He wanted to make us part of His family. Jesus' mission goes beyond salvation. Through Jesus, we have the privilege of being united with God, and it is a perfect union that is sealed by the blood of Jesus and the new covenant. Therefore, if you have surrendered your life to Jesus, you have access to a complete package. You have everything.

I do not think we understand the full impact of what Jesus did on the cross. We will not fully understand everything until we get to heaven. Think about it. We would be overjoyed if we understood what we have gained through Jesus' birth, death, and resurrection. We would be so excited that we would not be able to sit still.

Jesus prayed for unity among us, made possible through the glory the Father has bestowed upon Him. As we live for God, our lives reflect Jesus' glory that He has imparted to us. Someday, we will rule with Jesus when He comes in full glory and majesty. Satan will not be able to stop Him. He will rule as King of kings and Lord of lords. That is the goal of Jesus' mission.

CHAPTER TWENTY-TWO

COMPLETE UNITY

"I in them and you in me — so that they may be brought to complete unity. Then the world will know that you sent me and have loved them even as you have loved me." – John 17:23 NIV

There is no doubt that the fall of Adam and Eve brought chaos in God's family. For that reason, Jesus came as a second Adam to bridge the gap between humans and God. Jesus is the Redeemer. He came to repurchase us. Legally, Satan had the upper hand on humans when he tricked Adam and Eve into accepting his lies. In other words, God had to find a way to repurchase us by paying a considerable price with the precious blood of His Son Jesus. This extraordinary effort has granted humans a second chance of possessing what was once theirs.

The solution is in Jesus. Humans have a second chance through Jesus to unite with God. We can have everything we lost due to sin. Not only do we have an opportunity to have our relationship with God back, but we can now live in God, and God can live in us. We can unite with God through Jesus. That is what Jesus was praying about in this verse. By accepting Jesus as our Lord and Savior, He lives in us. Since the Father is in Jesus, by having Jesus living in us, we have the Father in us. That is a perfect, divine union that can only be made possible through a personal relationship with Jesus Christ - the Son of God.

Through this beautiful spiritual unity, the world will be able to have a glimpse of the divine design, which is intertwined in the love of God for His Son and those who have put their trust in Him as their Supreme Savior. It is not a small matter. That is an experience that should be given undivided attention because it has the key to eternal life.

CHAPTER TWENTY-THREE

JESUS' ETERNAL GLORY

"Father, I want those you have given me to be with me where I am, and to see my glory, the glory you have given me because you loved me before the creation of the world." – John 17:24 NIV

God's love did not start with the birth of Christ. God had manifested His great love before creation. Love is part of God's eternal plan.

Before creation, God loved Jesus. But, of course, Jesus is part of the Godhead. He agreed to humble Himself by becoming a man. While He was in the human body, He had to lay aside His privilege of being God. Keep in mind that Jesus was still God, but He did not enjoy all divine benefits while He was on earth. That was a willful decision because He wanted to experience all the suffering that comes with being human, and He did that by accepting to die on the cross for us.

Those of us who have surrendered ourselves to Jesus will have the opportunity to see Jesus' glory in all its splendor. Jesus prayed for that opportunity. Jesus' request shows that we will be with Him in eternity. We will see His glory and the love that the Father has for Him. It is truly awe-inspiring when we think about the joy of seeing Jesus in His full glory and majesty. There is nothing on earth that can compare with such experience.

It is an exclusive request. It only pertains to people who belong to Jesus. While God wants everyone to know Him, unfortunately, many people will choose otherwise. It is a terrible mistake to ignore God's invitation to participate in the eternal pursuit of happiness. I say an invitation because God does not choose to force anyone to accept His Son as Lord and Savior. This decision is personal. That is the way God chose to deal with humans. We have a will, and it is our prerogative to decide where we want to spend eternity.

CHAPTER TWENTY-FOUR

IF WE KNOW JESUS, WE KNOW THE FATHER

"Righteous Father, though the world does not know you, I know you, and they know that you have sent me." – John 17:25 NIV

While Jesus' mission was to set the captive free by taking upon Himself the sins of the world, He also introduced the heavenly Father to everyone. There is no freedom without the knowledge of the Creator of the universe. As it is often said, "knowledge is power." In the form of a divine encounter, a personal discovery of God is a liberating experience that opens the door to many spiritual blessings. Such blessings are matchless. There is nothing on earth that can equate the experience of being united with the Creator of the universe.

Jesus wanted His followers to understand that He was

not here to do His own will. Instead, He was sent by His Father to carry out a special mission. It was a mission of reconciling the world with the Godhead. By accepting to die on the cross for the sins of humanity, Jesus became the bridge that connects us with the heavenly Father.

As far as Jesus is concerned, the world does not understand Him. That is why there has been so much confusion about Jesus and what He represents. There have been many counterfeits.

Even Satan has been trying to elevate himself upon the throne of God. If you have a chance to study world religions, you will find out that there are bits and pieces of Christianity in many aspects of them. Even voodoo priests have tried to utilize the Christian Bible in their rituals. If you do not have a solid biblical education, you may not recognize false doctrines.

Today consider yourself blessed if you know that His Father sent Him. And if you have made Jesus your Lord and Savior, you are ready for the next big thing, which is the opportunity to live with the King of kings forever in the New Jerusalem. This truth must be the focus of everything you do. There is nothing more precious than knowing where you will spend eternity.

Jesus rejoiced that His disciples knew His origin and His mission, and He was excited about sharing His glory with them. To be with Jesus in glory should be the objective of everyone who believes. I hope you too are looking forward to it.

CHAPTER TWENTY-FIVE

JESUS MADE THE FATHER KNOWN

"I have made you known to them, and will continue to make you known in order that the love you have for me may be in them and that I myself may be in them." — *John 17:26 NIV*

To make Him known was one of the missions of Jesus. And He did that by making sure that His disciples knew who sent Him.

We must know who God is because we cannot experience His love if we do not know Him. Therefore, Jesus prayed that His disciples would share the love the Father has for Him. That is the love that compelled the heavenly Father to send His Son to die for us. It is love unspeakable and full of wonder.

As Christ's followers, we need to show God's love to the world so they may come to put their trust in Him. We cannot be effective witnesses for God if we do not display His love because unbelievers expect us to be authentic.

Keep in mind that you cannot truly love people if Jesus does not live in you. It is He who does the loving, not you.

ABOUT THE AUTHOR

Jean R. Lainé, a career public school educator with a fascinating story of struggle and triumph, is a Haitian-born American. Growing up in Haiti, Jean did not have the opportunity to attend school until age 13. However, despite his early educational setback, he completed several degrees in education and religion. Currently, he works as a curriculum specialist in the Putnam City school district

in Oklahoma City,
Oklahoma, where he lives.

BOOKS BY THIS AUTHOR

Twelve original Quotes for Your Sanity: A Monthly Source of Inspiration

These twelve original quotes are written to uplift your spirit when your soul is downcast. It is a monthly source of inspiration and motivation for your sanity. When you feel discouraged, depressed, or disoriented, you can turn to them for a dose of hope so that you can regain your bearing and forge ahead with your life.

Overcoming Adversity: Key to Victory and Success

Adversity can be anything in your life that keeps you from advancing toward your goals, including, but not limited to addictions, cultural differences, loss of loved ones, marital difficulties, divorce, diseases, fear, helplessness, hopelessness, linguistic limitations, poverty, physical handicaps, racism, worries, or anything that you would like to achieve in life. Still, you think that the decks are stacked against you.

Twelve Practical Reasons to Be Thankful: A Christian Approach to Year-Round Thanksgiving

In addition to all the delicious meals we enjoy around Thanksgiving, we have so much more for which to be thankful. I wrote this book to bring our attention to God, the Creator of the universe, and many priceless benefits that we can only find in Christ, the Savior.

In Search of Wisdom: A Daily Devotional Book

I wrote this devotional book to help you keep your mind on God daily. If you start and finish your year with an optimistic spin on life, you will likely experience success.

www.ingramcontent.com/pod-product-compliance
Lightning Source LLC
Chambersburg PA
CBHW031449040426
42444CB00007B/1033